GOING AGAINST THE GRAIN

A FORMULA TO CHANGE AND REVERSE SELF-DESTRUCTIVE BEHAVIORS

by

Mark Adams

authorHOUSE®

AuthorHouse™
1663 Liberty Drive, Suite 200
Bloomington, IN 47403
www.authorhouse.com
Phone: 1-800-839-8640

First published by AuthorHouse 4/11/2008

ISBN: 978-1-4343-8070-8 (sc)

Printed in the United States of America
Bloomington, Indiana

This book is printed on acid-free paper.

CONTENTS

PROLOGUE

This book is my contribution to help people change their self-destructive patterns of behavior. After twenty years of seeing people in my psychotherapy practice, I was able to formulate the answer to how any individual could "go against the grain." The book is separated into chapters in order to help the reader better understand the origins leading to destructive behavior patterns and the basis of my formula to effectuate change. The chapters will take you from childhood to adulthood in a simple but detailed manner. My aim in writing this book is to appeal not only to the average person, but also to the mental health professional. Hopefully both will consider themselves a team on the "healing" journey to healthy behavior.

I would like to thank my life partner and soul mate, Nancy, for helping me, or else I'm sure I would not have had the patience to complete this venture. I would also like to thank all in my Saddlebrooke writers group for letting me share my thoughts with them on this rewarding journey.

CHAPTER 1

BEGINNINGS AND EARLY CHILDHOOD

Childbirth

The age-old debate still continues over nature or nurture. Is personality inherited or developed environmentally? My purpose is not to try to answer this question, but to present the obvious. There may be some minimal behavioral characteristics that we inherit or, as they say, are in our genes. My view is that most personality traits are developed environmentally. I am speaking of the circumstances surrounding a person's development, whether in the early years or beyond. There is much discussion about what a child experiences at the moment of birth and even as a fetus before birth. We can say that some personality developments might be affected by a mother who is calm versus one who is anxious or hyperactive. We can also say that when a child is born, how he or she is held might also have an effect on its personality. Surely we can all relate some effect on a child's disposition in relation to how a mother, father, and/or caretakers interact with the child starting at birth. One of the examples many of us may be familiar with is the Rumanian experience. During the 1980s, in the country of Rumania, many parents had to give up children to the state due to poverty or political reasons. The state was promoting multiple births to increase the

1

population but was not providing resources. Therefore, many children were put in state orphanages and suffered emotionally due to the lack of affection. Although the children were being fed, clothed, and changed, they were not picked up and held. As a result of not experiencing any physically nurturing human contact, many children died. Therefore, we can see that not only personality can be affected environmentally, but that a child's very survival can depend on human contact and interaction. It is my view that we are all affected to a large degree by the environment, starting as a fetus and continuing after birth. The key words are, "to a large degree."

From my work with patients, I have found that the major effect on behavior occurs after birth and in conjunction with familial and environmental conditions. I do, though, want to be very clear that biology plays a major part in development when dealing with such syndromes as mental retardation, autism, Down syndrome, etc. Of course, even in the latter cases, environment and nurturing will play a significant role. Children are brought up in different political, social, and cultural environments, which have various effects, but the thrust of my formula rests mainly on degrees of trauma within one's family of origin and environment, on which I will elaborate in a later chapter.

Childhood

At the age of five or six, the main effect on a child's development is a result of his or her familial and environmental circumstances and events. Here is where little or much trauma may be experienced. Again, I refer to the "degree of trauma" as being important in a child's development. Of course, the type of trauma plays a significant role. In the next chapter, we will ponder the problem in deciding what may constitute trauma.

Let us now look at an example of a simple trauma that a child may experience. A five-year-old boy witnesses his father and mother in a heated argument, and the father begins to assault the mother. The boy attempts to help his mother and, as a result, is beaten by his father. We surely can recognize how painful that situation would be for the little boy and probably can agree that it was traumatic for him. It is common for people to want to forget painful experiences; therefore many of the traumas experienced by children may be buried or repressed in the subconscious. Although many of us go on to lead productive lives, these buried traumas may have an effect on how we handle relationships and the environment. We all have read or heard about financially successful people who suffer through many destructive relationships. We also are aware of many successful people who are haunted emotionally. Marilyn Monroe is an example of someone experiencing success while emotionally traumatized and haunted. Well, where do we go from here? I do think it's important to pause and deal with trauma in order to better clarify this anxious word; therefore the next chapter will start the process.

Chapter 2

Trauma

What is "trauma"? The dictionary defines trauma as "an emotional experience, or shock, which has a lasting psychic effect." Furthermore, the dictionary defines "psychic" as "beyond natural or known physical processes and, or, being sensitive to forces beyond the physical world." Here we can see a representation of events that can be buried deep in the psyche or subconscious. Therefore, any event causing anxiety, whether experienced as "one-time" or as "ongoing," can be designated as traumatic. The defining issue in this regard, I submit, is whether the event or events were experienced negatively or positively. Furthermore, the intensity of trauma seems to correlate with the amount of sadness or pain involved. In all the many years of my practice with patients affected by trauma, my experience has been that they generally found it hard to recall prior negative events but could easily remember and talk about their positive ones. Here is the beginning of the key to my formula for change, which I will discuss in detail later on. Negative trauma can be experienced as a one-time event or as ongoing. Typical experiences of one-time events are plane crashes, near-drownings, earthquakes, tsunamis, etc. Ongoing trauma can include sexual abuse, physical abuse, emotional abuse, etc. The latter can also occur once and be considered trauma. Examples of positive trauma are a roller coaster ride, learning how to swim, making love, eating chocolate, etc., all of which usually end happily. Many types of trauma are shame-based. Most trauma caused by abuse falls under this category, in contrast to a natural disaster or accident. While both produce feelings of powerlessness and lack of control, abuse trauma tends to leave a person with profound feelings of shame. I think it is important to point out that shame is not the same as guilt. Although both feelings involve self-reproach, guilt is the emotion we feel when we have harmed another person or lied to gain temporary advantage. Shame, on the other hand, is a sense of worthlessness where we hold ourselves in contempt, not so much for what we have done, but for who we are. We can alleviate pain from guilt by making amends, but shame needs healing to accept our essential self. Once a person becomes shame-based, the shame is self-triggering. Even when someone pays attention to us in a positive way, we might feel ashamed when we are shame-based. It would seem that a chapter about shame would be in order, but rather than that being the case, I feel that it's more important to understand how a person who has experienced abusive trauma can become shame-based and not be aware of it. For example, when sexual abuse occurs, whether to a young female or male, the abused person may think he or she deserves it. This is the "blaming the victim" syndrome. The victim wonders what it was about them that provoked the abuse. They ponder, "What did I do, or do wrong?" to provoke this awful action on the part of the perpetrator. Imagine a child experiencing one-time or ongoing abuse internalizing this thought and as a result becoming shame-based. Adults can also be affected, even though their abuse did not occur as children. Again, the degree and amount of abuse plays a major role.

An example of the "blame the victim" syndrome is a case that comes to mind in the Midwest, where a judge admonished a woman who was raped, telling her that she probably provoked the rape by wearing a miniskirt. Although an adult has a better capacity not to internalize shame, the woman who was raped can be made to feel she was inappropriate in public when in fact, she did nothing wrong. In the latter case, it's quite clear that the perpetrator broke the law and was clearly the one who was wrong. It's also quite clear how a respected person in power, such as the judge, can cause a person to feel a sense of shame. The reason I have emphasized shame as an important factor in dealing with trauma is that people may take on self-destructive behavior patterns in order to deal with repressed or suppressed feelings of shame. There are many people in prison as a result of acting out shame-based feelings. There are also many broken relationships as a result of this syndrome.

In a later chapter I will break down more specifically how trauma, whether abusive or otherwise, can produce various syndromes leading to self-destructive behavior patterns. The main thrust of this chapter on trauma is to introduce the concept that, to one degree or another, many of us experience a degree of post-traumatic stress, which then can affect our behavior. Post Traumatic Stress Disorder (PTSD) is generally caused by a prior trauma, or traumas, occurring in a person's lifetime that hasn't or haven't been resolved or dealt with. This is not to say we all have PTSD, but we might consider that PTSD could be a syndrome that is present in direct relation to the degree of trauma, or traumas, experienced in our past. To summarize, we can see that any discussion of trauma can be quite subjective. I feel, though, that it is important to have a basic understanding of trauma, since this area is the underpinning to support my formula that helps a person change their self-destructive behavior. Let us now go on to understand the developmental process presented in the next chapters before returning to this most important area.

Chapter 3

Latency

Chapter one discussed the role early childhood plays in the developmental process. This brings us to the latency period, which is the stage of personality development extending from about four or five years of age to the beginning of puberty. It is a time when sexual urges appear dormant. Also, at this period of pre-adolescence, any significant degree of introspection is lacking. Therapeutic interventions usually employed to get information or deal with feelings are of a play-therapy form of one model or another. Trauma experienced during this period can be confusing, both in form and in content. The child experiences the emotional effect of the trauma, but he or she is usually not able to express the feelings associated with it. In most cases, the feelings surrounding the traumatic event or events are internalized primitively without a cognitive language label attached to them. At an adult level, where we have learned all the feeling words associated with sad, difficult, or happy events, expression is not only possible, but understood. Denial that events have occurred, or will occur, can serve a purpose for an adult. The event can be too traumatic to face or to bear. With children, denial seems not to play a significant role. The child deals with events on more simple terms. By suppressing the feelings surrounding traumatic events, the child is able to continue actively within his or her environment, whether that is to stay still or to flee. Children are generally action oriented within their environment. This is probably a good survival technique that helps them adapt to circumstances that may occur suddenly or to general change.

The term "acting out" has been used to describe behavior by children. What children are generally doing when they are "acting out" are physically expressing their emotions. When a child experiences trauma, he or she usually has an internal emotional reaction, such as anger, fear, sadness, loss, excitement, etc., but acts on these feelings behaviorally. The child might even become immobilized, create a substitute personality, make believe he or she is elsewhere, reach for his or her favorite doll, etc., but an action is occurring, rather than a general cognitive experience of feelings associated with the trauma or traumas. Only in recent times have we become aware that it is important to help children verbalize their feelings associated with trauma as close in time as possible to the event or events. Unfortunately, in most cases this does not occur, and as a result, this has led to the present-day controversial discussion of "repressed memories." The controversy in this area surrounds memories of events adults become aware of that occurred in childhood. Many of these adults are suddenly confronted with the memory of a traumatic event or events that they were not aware of previously. An example is the mother of an eight-year-old girl. The mother, on the day of her daughter's eighth birthday, suddenly experiences severe symptoms and feelings of depression, anger, fear, etc. The mother seeks therapeutic help and, to her utter horror, discovers the memory that she was incested by her father when she was eight years old. In order for her to deal with the severity of the trauma, she not only repressed her feelings at the time of occurrence, but also the actual memory. The simple event that caused the mother's severe emotional reaction was her daughter's eighth birthday. The mother suddenly became an eight-year-old girl physically and emotionally, acting out those feelings she suppressed as a child. This could have occurred out of fear for her daughter experiencing the same event or simply becoming that little eight-year-old girl again herself. The mother, even though she didn't remember the event or events, still acted out her repressed feelings. To deal with these phenomena, some therapists employed hypnosis to help the person remember trauma, but that also created controversy. There were patients who, after experiencing hypnosis in therapy, claimed the therapist planted the memories. In some cases, patients recanted memories they had professed to recall during hypnosis in the therapeutic encounter. Many families suffered irreparable harm as a result of this experience. Therefore, I decided early on not to employ hypnosis in dealing with trauma treatment. Most of my patients, in time, were able to remember enough of the traumatic events, negating hypnosis as an aid. Rather than delve any further into this area where there is much controversy and discussion among clinicians and many books written, my main aim is to acquaint the reader with a basis for understanding the early developmental process leading up to my chapter dealing with changing self-destructive behavior.

In summary, this chapter on latency opens up the concept of repressed feelings and the "inner child," which I will explore extensively in a later chapter. How does this all lead to changes in self-destructive behavior? Please read on and, whether you feel change is needed or not, join me on this most interesting and stimulating journey, where next we explore puberty.

Chapter 4

Puberty

Puberty is the stage of development when the body starts to show significant changes. Physical characteristics may be compared to plants as they begin to bear flowers. Whereas young males may experience increased hair growth bodily, young females may notice enlargement of their breasts. This is also the stage at which persons are first capable of begetting or bearing children. The advent of increased interest in sexuality usually occurs with more frequency in this stage of development. What seems to be critical is a connection between desire and erotic arousal. In the latency period, although erotic arousal may be present or occur, desire for the opposite sex seems not to be as significant. For example, boys and girls in the latency period might express their dislike of the opposite sex, whereas in puberty, they start to experience the opposite. In fact, in some cultures the age of thirteen is symbolically celebrated as the advent of manhood or womanhood.

How, you may ask, could this information contribute to changing self-destructive behavior? This stage of development is most important, since this is where the teenage years start and self-identity is crucial. In fact, at this stage, many young people may begin to act self-destructively. Comparisons between peers, both physically and socially, usually begin in earnest at this time. While events and/or trauma that occurred prior to this period were emotionally confusing to the adolescent, now they are more cognitively understood. Whereas the adolescent during early childhood and latency was acting out their emotional reactions without understanding the causality, the young person experiencing puberty is better able to make that connection. Simply, the young person now "knows." This can lead to even more confusion, since when we know the causality of our emotional pain, it should be easier for us to act accordingly. When we are not able to release our emotions, for whatever reason, they usually are repressed and stored. For example, many children were physically, emotionally, or sexually abused during early childhood or latency and were prevented from acting out their primitive emotional reactions. They not only buried and stored those feelings without making any connection to the abusive acts, but they may have acted out their feelings socially in other ways, such as poor grades in school, bullying, poor hygiene, anxiety, depression, extreme shyness, isolation, etc., all of which generally are destructive to the self and /or others. In contrast, when the young person in puberty experiences, or continues to experience, the abusive event or events, he or she is making the connection between the feelings and causality.

What is, therefore, the difference that contributes to self-destructive behavior on the part of the adolescent or young person? While both become self-destructive in their acting-out behavior, the knowledge of causality differs. Once the understanding of the causality of emotional pain is experienced, then "shame" begins to play a significant role in personality development. Whereas in latency and early childhood, shame was not cognitively present due to a lack of connecting the event to the emotion, in puberty shame now starts to be part of the expression by the young person, who then may act out self-destructively. Again, that behavior may be failing grades, drug and/or alcohol use, violence, self-abuse, isolation, etc., all resulting in social trouble and/or pain and punishment for the young person. Also, as the young person experiences social or environmental problems, he or she may continue to be self-destructive. This may be due to the degree of trauma experienced in his environment and the amount of shame, therefore, that occurs as a result.

The issue of shame was also discussed in a prior chapter. The reason is to emphasize how shame resulting from abuse can be internalized and lead to a "blame the victim" syndrome by the abused person. This reinforces self-destructive behavior as the abused person feels he or she is worthless and deserves to be punished. Of course, there are traumas people experience that are not abusive. Examples were referred to in a prior chapter that included tornados, tsunamis, earthquakes, air disasters, war injuries, etc. Although these traumas may not result in self-destructive behavior, the injury to the psyche can be dramatic unless dealt with. In general, if trauma is not treated, the person may feel victimized whether or not abuse occurred. Many trauma victims internalize the syndrome "why me"? This may not lead to feeling shame, but it does tend to contribute to the feeling of victimization, which could also lead to self-destructive behavior. In a later chapter, when I explain the formula to change behavior, the issue of general trauma will again be discussed in order to fully clarify how all traumas, unless treated, can lead to self-destructive behavior. Now let us go on to the teenage years.

CHAPTER 5

TEENAGE YEARS

The teenage years, from thirteen to twenty, are most significant in terms of identity. Whereas personality traits are developed throughout the early years of childhood and puberty, the search for identity in relation to peers and the environment is a central theme for the teenager. Social and environmental risk and discovery are experienced on a daily basis, and behavior is an essential part of how the teenager is affected and affects others. Although this period is one where verbal expression is operative, behavioral action usually takes precedence. Since the teenager can verbally interact and has insight, trauma can be treated. Unfortunately, the search for self-identity complicates trauma treatment, in that the teenager finds it hard to focus on any material that doesn't address his or her identity. Nevertheless, an attempt needs to be made to help the teenager deal with trauma in order to prevent destructive behavior.

In a later chapter I address how trauma treatment, in the context of my formula to change self-destructive behavior, can be applied to adolescents, teenagers, and adults. Although the process may differ for each age group, the general approach and result desired is the same. The underlying emotion that seems to be the most active for many teenagers is fear. Past trauma can contribute to the teenager viewing his or her environment as threatening. Acting from fear can lead the teenager to self-destructive behavior. One of the most common fears teenagers experience is the fear of rejection. This, of course, may be felt in different degrees by each teenager according to prior experiences and trauma. Many teenagers who have experienced abuse have severe low self-images. This can lead to behaviors which, when self-destructive, reinforce their low self-image. Another fear is one of safety. Again, when trauma has been experienced, a person's future safety comes into question. An example may be the very neighborhood where the teenager grew up. There may be a rule on the streets or in school that if you don't belong to a particular gang or clan you will not fit in. The drive for most teenagers is to fit in, especially more so by those who have experienced abusive trauma. Many teenagers will drink and drug in order to loosen up so that they will feel more comfortable socially. This can become quite self-destructive when the teenager, who may have a low self-image, needs the mood-altering substance, rather than it being experimental and part of the "rite of passage."

Anger is another emotion that leads to severe self-destructive behavior. A person who experiences trauma, especially when not treated, usually has a reservoir of anger that may erupt in harmful ways. Many teenagers who have experienced abuse are walking time bombs who may release their anger "sideways." I want to be clear about the phrases "rite of passage" and "sideways." "Rite of passage" refers to the experimental phases that most people go through during adolescence. Many try alcohol but do not necessarily become self-destructive. "Sideways" is when we act out hurtfully in situations that do not fit the action. We are acting out feelings that occurred due to other circumstances. Again, at this stage the teenager is more action oriented in dealing with emotions rather than verbally expressive and insightful.

The purpose of this chapter is to bring an awareness of how early self-destructive behavior begins. We can all see how adolescents and teenagers can act out self-destructively as a way to deal with their emotions. When those emotions, caused by trauma, have been repressed throughout adolescence and into adulthood, their eventual expression can be quite destructive. This brings us to adulthood. Although the teenage years are ideally the ones where trauma should be treated, the teenager is usually not receptive. Therefore, the adult years are the ones where treatment is usually sought, especially when destructive behaviors are serious enough to warrant attention. Let us now discuss adulthood in the next chapter, as we continue the journey to emotional health.

CHAPTER 6

ADULTHOOD

Adulthood characterizes the years starting where the teenage years end, that being around twenty-one years of age. Our society recognizes twenty-one as the age where a person is legally responsible for their actions. Although eighteen is the age generally thought of as legal age, there are behaviors restricted to age twenty-one in many locales, such as smoking, drinking, gambling, etc. In fact, before the age of twenty-one, a person's parents can possibly be held responsible for their debts. Of course, there are many teenagers who are mental adults long before the age of twenty-one. They have matured for various reasons, which may be due to environmental and biological circumstances referred to in a prior chapter. In many locales, society treats sixteen years of age as when a teenager may request to become emancipated, depending on their parent's consent, to live independently. In any event, since the previous chapter covered the teenage years, the chapter on adulthood can be seen as starting at twenty-one years of age, the magic age of total legality. My aim in focusing on the latter information was not to be confusing or redundant, but to point out that the boundaries of maturity are not as clearly defined as those between latency, puberty, and the teenage years.

Adulthood starts to represent the years when a person becomes insightful or more willing to look inward and reflect upon the course of his or her behavior. In fact, since adults are considered responsible for their actions, destructive behavior may result in their being compelled to address such behavior by going for therapeutic help. This is clearly experienced in the court system when addressing addictions, drunk driving, familial neglect, and abuse, etc. Many judges now compel people to address their mental health as part of the legal and judicial process by remanding them to treatment. Of course, it is one thing to be remanded for treatment and another to seek it voluntarily. In my experience, there were better results in treatment with those who attended voluntarily, rather than those who were remanded by the legal system. Nevertheless, once someone started to address their behavior through psychotherapy, it was quite evident that a whole new healthy approach to life was possible. Adulthood was the period of time when people dramatically changed their behavior. When adults came to treatment, they usually did so independently and did not need to be transported by their families. This was in stark contrast to adolescents and teenagers who needed familial transportation and involvement. In fact many young adults, usually beginning at the age of seventeen and eighteen, were in the healthy process of separation from their family of origin and seeking support in their endeavor. An entire chapter could be devoted to a confusing and emotional time for the teenager and the family focusing on separation issues. The thrust of this chapter is to point out that it's never too late to address behavioral change. In my experience, though, it's more productive when you do so in adulthood. This does not mean that if you are an adolescent or teenager reading this book, you cannot be helped. In fact, the very act of your reading this book demonstrates the maturity necessary to participate in achieving emotional and behavioral health. This chapter on adulthood opens up the process necessary to achieve healthy behaviors. My next chapter will address syndromes people exhibit that tend to lead to self-destructive behavior. It is a well-needed chapter before we pursue the formula for change, so read on and let us continue on the road to healthy behavior.

CHAPTER 7

SYNDROMES

Before discussing the formula to change self-destructive behavior, it is important to note the various syndromes, symptoms, or so-called disorders that people are plagued with. The most common are anxiety, depression, obsession, hyperactivity, addictions, impulsiveness, etc. A syndrome is defined as a group of disease symptoms commonly found or associated with one another. A disorder is defined as a state of confusion, disease, or ailment. There is no doubt that we all have feelings in association with those syndromes mentioned above. It is only when those feelings become so excessive and pronounced so as to seriously affect our behaviors that we may refer to them as syndromes or disorders. Anxiety and depression are two of the most common symptoms that may lead to self-destructive behavior. Pronounced anxiety may produce panic attacks, which can lead to problems in employment or general social withdrawal. Depression can lead to a sense of doom and the extensive use of drugs and alcohol to deal with one's feelings. Of course, there are psychiatric medications that can be quite helpful in severe cases. Whether the symptoms are mild or pronounced, they surely can affect a person's feelings when interacting with his or her environment. In short, our actions are usually in direct correlation with our feelings, and when those feelings, whether repressed or aware, are overactive, self-destructive behavior can occur. Addictions, such as drugs, alcohol, food, gambling, etc., are usually quite self-destructive.

In my experience, addictions are a way of dealing with these overactive feelings mentioned previously. The substances used initially may have been taken to soothe those feelings but eventually resulted in the addiction. My aim is not to extensively explore each syndrome or symptom, but to open up the notion that feelings are at the core of our behaviors. Since the object of this book is to help people change self-destructive behavior, the focus is not to dwell on the syndromes, but on how we accomplish this change. Therefore, it is important to note that syndromes, symptoms, and/or disorders usually result from prior trauma.

As stated in a previous chapter, untreated trauma can leave a person with repressed feelings that are acted on behaviorally and/or are symptom addictive. This is not to say that all syndromes or disorders are a result of trauma. There are some that may be biological in nature, such as schizophrenia and bipolar disorders. Even chronic depression has been thought of as primarily biological. It is unfortunate that those people who have biological disorders may also have suffered trauma, such as sexual abuse, etc. Surely it is much more complicated to treat those persons for Post Traumatic Stress Disorder (PTSD) than it is the general population. My focus in this book is with the general population, but my formula can be applied to any population by adjusting the approach appropriately. I hope this chapter has been fruitful in exploring how the various syndromes, such as anxiety and depression, when overactive, can lead to self-destructive behavior. As stated previously, I deem it most important to deal with repressed feelings in order to make behavioral changes. This leads us to our next chapter, which may be quite controversial but most important in laying the groundwork for my formula. Therefore, read on, brave souls, and discover your "child within."

CHAPTER 8

THE CHILD WITHIN

This chapter, although some may consider it controversial, covers a concept that is at the core of my formula. To understand and accept this concept, I ask you to be subjective in your approach. I submit that all of us have a "child within" that is reactive in social and environmental situations. The concept of a "child within" can also be referred to as the "inner child." In the prior chapters of early childhood and latency I discussed how emotions related to traumas and how the very trauma itself could be repressed. During these periods of time, since children are more action oriented than insightful, there would be a strong tendency for the child to repress feelings rather than express them. Therefore, it is my view that those feelings remain in the subconscious and are acted on in relation to the degree of severity and type of trauma experienced. Teenagers may also repress feelings when unable to express them for one reason or another, so the concept of "inner child" does not necessarily end at puberty. When abuse has occurred and the feelings associated with this type of trauma are repressed, usually the victim can be quite self-destructive behaviorally.

One example of how the "inner child" reaction may play out is of a child abandoned by his or her mother or father at the age of five or six. The child, unless therapeutically treated, represses his or her feelings of terror, fear, rejection, etc. An adult, and even a teenager, can overreact to situations where they may feel abandoned or rejected. This could happen in a social situation where simple rejection occurs normally, such as the opposite sex refusing overtures (Would you like to dance? How about a date?). The adult who overreacts usually is feeling like that "injured child" again who was hurt earlier in life and repressed the feelings at the time. As a result of a simple rejection, the adult who is overreacting may then become self-destructive and compound the situation. The rejection would confirm his or her feelings of worthlessness and/or powerlessness experienced as a child. You may ask the question, how could a person react as a child in adult situations? The degree and extent of trauma suffered and the repression of feelings associated with the trauma or traumas will affect reactions in social and environmental situations. Many persons have ended up in prison as a result of their violent reactions to a social situation. They may have repressed feelings of rage due to their being abused, neglected, or abandoned as children. Hitler experienced a horribly abusive childhood. We could definitely say that Hitler was not only genocidal but also self-destructive. Am I saying that Hitler was acting out his "inner child"? Whether he was or not, we do know that he never had any therapeutic treatment for his childhood abuse.

This brings me back to the concept of the "child within." Again, I repeat, we all have an "inner child." Some of us may have a healthier "inner child," which was nurtured and did not experience any significant trauma. Others have experienced significant trauma, whether through abuse or otherwise. I submit that those of us who were nurtured well and experienced little trauma may very well react better to environmental and social situations than those who were not nurtured well and repressed significant trauma. How that happens seems to be somewhat primitive, in that we all need to react quickly to most situations. If we have been injured as children, then our immediate reaction could be negative. Again, that depends on whether there has been any treatment and "healing" for past trauma. I will leave the subject of treatment and "healing" for a future chapter and hope your "inner child" is reacting well to this concept. Let us return to the subject of trauma once again, since it plays such an important role in affecting our behavior.

CHAPTER 9

TRAUMA REVISITED

How can trauma, which I introduced in chapter three, produce various syndromes leading to self-destructive behavior patterns? In the prior chapter we discussed how the "inner child" can be affected by trauma. In this chapter, let us take a further view of trauma. Again, we need to be somewhat subjective, since all trauma experienced may not be similar. What are some of the traumatic experiences that can contribute to producing the various syndromes we discussed in chapter eight? Abuse, in its various forms, surely can result in the victim's internalization of intense feelings. The three main forms of abuse are sexual, physical, and emotional. We discussed in a prior chapter how the person experiencing the abuse can adapt a victimization approach to life. The abused person's behavior can reflect this approach when dealing with the environment and/or social situations. Negative occurrences may be felt as deserved by the victims, since they are convinced that they caused, or contributed to, the original abuse in some way. These types of trauma, unless treated, usually result in the victim continuing to behave self-destructively when dealing with the environment or interacting in a social situation. The feelings of fear, terror, rage, powerlessness, etc., are usually all felt when experiencing abuse but can go unexpressed and, in fact, may have been repressed. We need to bear this in mind, since unexpressed feelings are at the core of my formula to change self-destructive behavior, which we will discuss in a future chapter.

Other traumas are those that produce the feelings mentioned above but may not result in the person feeling victimized or in reducing their self-image. These traumas may be seen as random happenings of being in the wrong place at the wrong time. A plane crash, train derailing, roller coaster accident, fire, terrorist incident, war, etc., all are examples of random happenings. Of course, the "if only" syndrome can result where the victim could feel that they didn't do enough or could have done something different to affect the event. This can leave the survivor of the traumatic occurrence with the feelings of self-loathing, again possibly resulting in self-destructive behavior. Here, too, unless the feelings experienced in conjunction with the trauma are expressed, they may become repressed and have a future effect on the victim's behavior. Ongoing trauma, in many instances not seen as such by the victims, can be much more damaging than single events. What is most common in this area are people who grow up without any significant physical or emotional nurturing. In the many years of my practice, the most common verbal expression patients shared with me was the lack of love by their parents, whether physical, emotional, or verbal. In fact, many of my patients did not even regard this as unusual. Since they had entered therapy addressing some behavioral or interpersonal problem, their focus was on solving same. In the process of taking family histories, which was a general rule of mine before undertaking treatment, I would find that many of my patients experienced hardly any nurturing during their childhood. In fact, many had experienced negative and critical messages within their family environment. This would be an example of ongoing trauma, whether or not recognized by the victim. The feelings associated with lack of love and negative messages can be anger, depression, anxiety, etc., and when repressed, as they usually are not allowed to be expressed in abusive environments, may end up causing self-destructive behavior by the victim.

Of course, the subject of trauma could fill a book by itself. Rather than discussing it in depth, the main reason I have only devoted two short chapters to trauma is to emphasize the importance it plays relating to self-destructive behavior. The next chapter will start to deal with destructive behaviors and their possible patterns, so let us read on while we continue our journey to emotional and physical health.

CHAPTER 10

SELF-DESTRUCTIVE BEHAVIOR PATTERNS

What are some of the areas that best describe examples of self-destructive behavior? What comes to mind undoubtedly is what most of my patients expressed initially as their presenting problem. The common problems were in the area of relationships. Human beings are very similar to most living organisms, in that we require social involvement with others. The problem arises when the involvement becomes destructive, whether to oneself or another. Destructive patterns can occur and cause a person to hopefully seek help in order to make change. In most cases, the person cannot identify the causation leading to the pattern and therefore is at a loss to accomplish healthy change. One common pattern is the fear of intimacy. A person who lacked nurturing as a child or suffered parental abandonment, whether actual or emotional, can surely develop trust issues. A person who was constantly criticized as a child may also develop over reactive fears of rejection. The pattern resulting from those circumstances can be many attempts at close relationships without success. Many broken marriages and/or relationships can occur as a result. A tremendous amount of testing can drive away the very person one may desire. A person who was abused as a child may feel the need to test the person they desire so as to really prove they are loved, since as a child they were surely given the message of being unlovable. These tests can then become self-destructive in that the desired person can't pass them since they are too hard or impossible to accomplish. The result is that the relationship ends with either one blaming the other and no recognition of the dysfunction probably prevalent. A common example of testing is the phrase, "If she or he really loved me they would do what I like," even though that desire might be dysfunctional or destructive. "If he loved me, he would listen to me and do whatever I want." "If she loved me, she would join me in drinking or smoking." I guess we could go on and on and start to possibly remember or substitute our own examples of dysfunctional tests.

Another pattern is one of confusion. Since many people have come from environments that were depressing or anxiety provoking, they find it hard to function in stable or serene surroundings. These people either tend to create havoc and thrive on excitement or, on the other end of the spectrum, withdraw and become couch potatoes.

There are many people with repressed rage who have acted out their feelings by getting into physical fights. Of course, this usually ends up as destructive, not only to the person, but to others as well. When patterns continue to develop in these areas, many times the legal institutions may become involved. The other side of the coin is self-abuse. Depression is usually unexpressed anger, and many people take their anger out on themselves by physical self-abuse or the ultimate self-destructive behavior, that being suicide. Some people actually survive suicidal patterns, but unfortunately many do not. Of course, this is the extreme, and usually psychiatric intervention with medication can help. I will discuss this important issue again in chapter fourteen.

You might want to stop at this point and give some thought to your own possible self-destructive patterns of behavior. In my own life, the focus was on a lack of trust and fears of intimacy. You're right if you perceived my problem as starting in childhood due to emotional abuse. In addition to witnessing numerous patients successfully reversing destructive behaviors, I also took the opportunity to test my theory by personally experiencing treatment, which gave me additional confidence and motivation to write this book and share my formula. In order to change, we must first recognize the need for change. This chapter has been devoted to opening up the concept of how behavior may be self-destructive and the dysfunctional patterns that can develop. Now, brave reader, let us read on and discover how we may recognize the need for change. Of course, if you started reading this book out of curiosity and are now up to this point, you probably have recognized your own possible need for change. Read on, though, so we can together discuss the formula to change self-destructive behavior.

CHAPTER 11

NEEDED CHANGE

In prior chapters, when referring to behavioral change we discussed the environment as being the catalyst. That is, when behavior would cause a problem, the legal system might intervene, and as a result, the person would seek help to ensure more functional behavior. An example might be a DWI (driving while intoxicated) citation forcing a person into treatment. In my experience, most people will resist change. Even dysfunctional lifestyles, when repetitive, can become habitual. Unfortunately, they eventually may lead to doom. An extreme example would be an eight-hundred-pound person. Although the person knows the behavior of overeating is leading to his or her early doom, the behavior continues and in many cases escalates. In one of my visits to a hospital, I came upon a patient who was smoking even though he had a severe case of lung disease. I guess we could say that these are extreme examples where disease is present, but they do exhibit a common defense we all use, which is "denial." There is an old street saying that "denial is not a river in Egypt." Well it sure isn't, but denial can serve a purpose for dysfunctional behavior to continue.

To further illustrate how dramatic a role denial plays, let me share a personal experience. I had a conversation with my brother about a year before his death. We discussed his excessive smoking and sugar habits.

His doctor had told him to stop smoking and to watch his sweets intake due to his diagnosis of high blood pressure and diabetes. I pleaded with him to stop smoking and reduce his excessive sugar consumption. My brother retorted, "So I'll live ten years less, but at least I will enjoy my life." He was in his early sixties at the time, and he visualized living until ninety, and with ten years chopped off his concept was to surely reach eighty. I told him he was in denial in order to smoke and enjoy sweets and that he might die much sooner unless he listened to the doctor. He laughed. Well, he died a year later as a result of complications from a stroke, which was due to his negligence in caring for his high blood pressure and diabetes. He surely didn't want to die in his early sixties, but "denial" enabled him to satisfy his desire for immediate gratification. I don't intend to make this a chapter on denial but feel it is very important to point out the stronghold this mechanism has on our own psyche. When we are dealing with disease, such as alcoholism, eating disorders, drug addiction, etc., extensive treatment is needed to break down the denial.

In most cases, though, we are not dealing with disease but with general self-destructive patterns of behavior mentioned in the prior chapter. Unfortunately, in my experience as a practitioner, most people do not change unless they are "miserable enough" to do so. As discussed previously, continued dysfunctional relationship patterns could become the catalyst that motivates a person to seek treatment. This also applies to the alcoholic or eating-disorder person. Their dysfunctional behaviors could motivate other people to force them to change. A national example is Betty Ford, the wife of our former president Gerald Ford. He bravely confronted her alcohol abuse with what they referred to as a "family intervention," resulting in her seeking treatment and starting the Betty Ford Center, a well-known alcohol treatment facility.

If you are now reading this book, you may be one of those who do not have to become very miserable in order to change. You may have picked up the book out of curiosity, or you may be a person who is desperate for a solution. My formula is available for all, whether desperate, miserable, or just curious. First there needs to be a desire for change. This may come about as a result of the recognition of a need to change. Whether or not this is so, what is most important is the desire to change. Even if you arrived at this point through curiosity and you now recognize a need for change, a desire is necessary in order to eventually accomplish it. In my brother's case, he did not have any desire to change. He had recognition of his problem, but not a desire. Once we act on the desire, there is a good possibility of results. That is not to say that the person who is remanded to treatment will not get the results. At least he or she is in treatment and has a chance to change. For those not remanded, which most are, you do need a desire to change or you will probably not start the process at all. We are nearly there, to "the formula for change." The next chapter will set the stage for my presentation of "the formula for change." Before discussing my presentation, the next chapter is most important in the process, so let us proceed on our joint journey to emotional health.

CHAPTER 12

HEALING AND SUPPORT

Before describing the process necessary relating to the formula for change, which will be the focus of the next chapter, it's very important to understand the concept of healing. In prior chapters we discussed how intense feelings may have been repressed when experiencing a trauma or traumas. We also discussed how those repressed feelings could simmer and boil below the surface and end up causing destructive behavior, both to the self and others. How does healing enter the picture? If you cut yourself accidentally, in most cases there would be a short period of healing. If you had an operation of some type, there would follow a period of healing. How does this compare to a person who has experienced trauma and repressed intense unexpressed feelings? I submit that the concept is very simple. Just as we heal from physical wounds, so do we need to heal from emotional wounds. If the person who was cut or operated on did not attend to their wounds, healing would not take place. In fact, decay might result. This, I submit, is what happens when intense feelings are repressed as a result of trauma. Therefore, healing is an essential concept of my formula to change self-destructive behavior. When people are injured emotionally, whether by perpetrators or accidentally, healing needs to take place. In a prior chapter I briefly discussed PTSD (Post Traumatic Stress Disorder) and how a person who suffers trauma may thereafter develop various symptoms that can cause self-destructive behavior.

A prime example of this syndrome occurred after the Viet Nam War. Many veterans who suffered severe traumatic experiences went untreated and, as a result, ended up with problems such as addictions, broken marriages or relationships, mental disorders, violent encounters, suicide, etc. Fortunately, many Viet Nam veteran therapeutic groups were formed where they could get treatment and support for their PTSD. I consider that "their healing." Within those groups, which were professionally led, the veterans shared their own traumatic experience during the Viet Nam War. They would also share their feelings about those experiences that may have occurred many years previously. Most had repressed those feelings at the time the trauma or traumas occurred. An important dynamic of the group sharing was the care and support of fellow veterans who surely could empathize with each other. A lot of simmering and boiling was probably going on within them for many years before treatment, contributing to self-destructive behavior. Am I submitting that we all have a touch of PTSD? Not necessarily. Believe it or not, some people have not been subject to serious trauma. Intense feelings were not repressed by them; therefore they may not need to heal. I do submit, though, that many of us are walking time bombs. Hopefully this book can help defuse those time bombs by sharing how we can heal past wounds.

Before going forward and describing the healing process, which I will endeavor to do in the next chapter, it is most important to stop here and discuss "support." You may continue to read, but please return to the concept before attempting my "healing formula." The concept of support simply means that you are hopefully not alone on your journey to emotional health. A loving mate, friend, relative, support groups, etc., could suffice. It's important that you are not completely alone in the world when you initiate the process of healing. If there is no one, as for many of us there is not, then consider a support group. Since most of have come from dysfunctional families, there is surely a support group that will fit. Some good examples are twelve-step support groups, which only ask for minimal voluntary contributions to attend and are not professionally led. They are not therapy groups but are places where a person can share feelings with caring support from others. These groups are anonymous, in that you may only share your first name, and are not judgmental. In many ways they are similar to the healthy family of origin, which many of us were denied. Most are listed in local telephone books and on the Internet. Some examples of twelve-step groups are CODAP (codependents anonymous) Alanon, Naranon, Oanon, etc.

In my final chapter I will return to this most important area, since I consider it essential for success. In fact, I suggest a person not attempt healing without addressing this issue first. Read on, though, for the next chapter starts to describe the formula to change self-destructive behavior.

CHAPTER 13

"TELLING THE STORY"

Now, brave reader, you have arrived at the core of my formula to change self-destructive behavior. Our journey together has mainly covered the developmental areas and the process leading up to this most important chapter. "Telling the story" is as simple as it sounds, but does need a professional witness each time it occurs. To set the stage, let me expand on what I mean by "telling the story." In prior chapters, when we discussed PTSD, we focused on trauma as causation. It is generally agreed that, when dealing with traumatic events, a form of debriefing is necessary in order to avoid severe emotional aftereffects. Two recent examples are the plane crash off the Long Island, New York, coast and the 9/11 disaster. Mental health professionals were sent immediately to the disaster sites so that survivors and helpers could both be debriefed. This was their "telling the story" of what had just occurred. This act helps the person not repress the feelings associated with the traumatic event. Two things are accomplished. The surviving victim and the helper, both of whom have experienced the disaster, get to "tell the story" to a witness. As I previously stated, it's most important that the witness be a mental health professional. It also goes without saying that the mental health professional has prior training in trauma therapy. In fact, it is recommended that those mental health professionals who do the debriefing get similar help thereafter, since it is quite traumatic to participate in trauma therapy.

All of the latter is to open up the concept of "telling the story" as being critical in dealing with trauma recovery and healing. This concept is somewhat similar to the process of "confession" in Catholicism. There, the person enters a confessional booth and tells a traumatic story to his or her priest, who is on the other side of a partition to protect the anonymity of the "confessor." The focus here is mainly on sin, but the process indirectly deals with the person releasing their feelings about the event or events related. Of course, this is not a substitute for dealing with trauma recovery, where the concept of sin is not a focus and the storyteller sees the witness. What is most important, though, is that "telling the story" is the key to healing and recovery. I am simply referring to the details of the traumatic event or events as the survivor or helper experienced. Most of the cases I have dealt with in therapy have been those persons who have experienced abusive trauma and had not had the opportunity to "tell their story." In fact, this concept was foreign to them. Most had come to therapy in order to deal with destructive behavior in one form or another.

Before leading my patients on the path to "telling their story," I made sure they had a support system in one form or another, as I related in chapter twelve. My past experience had led me to believe that almost any other path to help people change destructive behaviors would only be a Band-Aid. Many could not remember all of their past traumatic events. That was alright. In "telling the story" again and again, most were able to recall more and more of what had occurred. It was not my job to embellish the story, but just to be a witness and sensitively help them release their repressed feelings that occurred at the time of the trauma or traumas. It doesn't mean that the person had to describe every detail of the actual event. In fact, that could contribute to further victimize the person. The main focus is to help the release of repressed feelings so that "healing" can occur. It's sort of like having an ulcer festering in your stomach for years. You then discover successful treatment with an antibiotic for the first time and, finally, healing takes place. Well, that's what "telling the story" is all about. When it's done in the structured way I will present, healing can surely take place. Only then, after healing, can behavioral change occur.

This chapter opens up the key to my formula. I do not want to oversimplify my concept of "telling the story," nor do I want to over-detail it. Keeping it simple is the best way to approach the healing process. I want to emphasize once again, though, that "telling the story" to just "anybody" could be more harmful than healing. There is an old saying, "Buyer beware." In my next chapter I will describe the process and structure for the success of my formula, so let us continue our brave journey on the road to healthy behavior.

CHAPTER 14

RECOGNIZING THE KEYS

If you have been brave enough to have come this far, you surely deserve a structural process to help you on your journey to change self-destructive behavior. I'm sure we do not want to lose sight of the goal. Many a book has led readers on a complicated journey to nowhere. That is not my desire. Just as I have taken this journey, with much emotional pain and destructive behavior prior to healing, so you too can come out the other side and experience emotional health and functional behavior. Let us now briefly review the prior chapters.

Chapter one dealt with the beginnings and early childhood, where we started to discover how children could repress their feelings in relation to trauma. Chapter two dealt with the latency period of childhood between the approximate ages of six or seven and up to puberty at about eleven or twelve. We devoted two chapters to trauma in order to present a simple understanding of this area. We then went on to puberty, the teenage years, and adulthood and explained how the effect of trauma as well as the treatment may differ in each of those stages. We discussed the syndromes that could result due to traumatic environments, such as anxiety, panic, obsessive compulsiveness, hyper-vigilance, depression, etc. In the chapter on syndromes, we discussed how persons could develop social phobias that could lead to self-destructive behavior. We devoted an entire chapter to our "child within," which focused on the "injured child" as a result of suffering a trauma or traumas. This opened up the concept of "healing" the "injured child." We visited some of the destructive behavior patterns that could occur, and the reader was presented with a chance for them to possibly identify some of their own patterns of behavior. We went on to discuss in chapter eleven the need for change and, in chapter twelve, the important concept of "healing" and "support." This brought us to the very important chapter thirteen, where we discussed in detail the concept of "telling the story." This all now brings us to the present chapter, which will recognize and describe the keys to successful treatment.

Hopefully, at this point you have recognized some of your own destructive behavior patterns. Even if you have not, but do experience discomfort, you may still want to follow the process in your pursuit to change and/or reverse self-destructive behavior. Here are the keys to successful treatment for healing:

1) Be sure to have a support system in place as discussed in chapter twelve. If not, you can still go ahead with number two below, but be sure not to start "telling the story" until you do.

2) Find a sensitive mental health therapist. This can be found through recommendation by your doctor, your insurance carrier, a friend, or local county services. You can go to an agency, such as the YMCA, YMHA, family services, etc. What is most important is the type of professional who does the treatment. My strong recommendation is that the professional be a licensed social worker or psychologist. He or she can also be a psychiatrist, but generally they do not focus on talk therapy. My preference is a licensed clinical social worker. Their training usually focuses on people being affected by their environment rather than being individually deficient. Remember when I

said "Buyer beware"? This is the most important part of the treatment. Making the right choice in picking your therapist is critical. This person will be your "witness" and help you heal. You are now an educated consumer. You can interview the therapist and make sure that he or she will be a sensitive and caring listener who has the opportunity to help you "heal." You can bring a copy of this book to the interview so as to feel less intimidated by the "professional." It's important, though, not to let the therapist try to change the process. Hopefully, that will not occur. Many therapists may try to use their own methodology. You have the right as a consumer to interview your therapist prior to treatment and choose to continue, or not to continue, at any time in the process. Remember, this book can be your guide.

3) Begin the therapeutic process. A book that survivors of child sexual abuse may want to purchase as part of the process is entitled *Courage to Heal* by Ellen Bass, but I again strongly suggest that you do not start the "healing" without support and professional help.

4) Be sure the therapist has access to a psychiatrist. This is not to put fear into the treatment, but to face the possibility that the "healing" process can be quite traumatic. In most cases, I have found that people could "heal" well without the need of medication. In the rare case that a person may need medication temporarily, a psychiatric referral during continuing treatment may be needed for that purpose. In some cases a person may be on medication already and have a psychiatrist before seeking a therapist to be their witness in "healing."

5) It would be helpful to have a physical examination before starting treatment in order to deal with any physical problems

or diseases that need attention, such as high blood pressure, diabetes, etc.

6) What about changing destructive behavior? Don't worry; I do not intend to abandon or leave you now. In my next and last chapter, which is the title of this book, *Going Against the Grain*, I will bring this all together so you and your "witness" can both go on your glorious journey to emotional health. Read on, brave survivor, as we all "go against the grain"!

CHAPTER 15

GOING AGAINST THE GRAIN

Self-destructive behavior that began as a result of a dysfunctional environment can become habitual. Even though you know the behavior is destructive, you may feel compelled to continue it. In many cases it can become "second nature," which, even though the behavior produces discomfort, feels natural. Smoking, overeating, and excessive drinking are common examples of self-destructive actions that become very hard habits to break. Continuing self-destructive relationships with highly critical partners may feel hurtful, but also may have become habitual. Destructive habits usually start in our early years and continue to blossom as we age. They all seem to feed into our hurt "inner child" and, although they may feel soothing or exciting at the moment, they are generally injurious to our emotional and physical health. The man or woman who was abused as a child acts out the self-loathing messages given to him or her by the abusing environment. "Going against the grain" simply means changing behavior that may feel good at the time but is surely self-destructive. In chapter fourteen I outlined the steps to take that start the process of change. In this chapter I am bringing it all together so the reader can better understand not only how to "go against the grain," but to believe in the process to do so. Life can be quite simple and complicated at the same time. Most people who have been successful in their endeavors did not get there overnight. The accomplished opera singer spent many years perfecting his or her craft. Most of us can look back and recognize that it took years to improve whatever endeavor we might presently continue to pursue. There usually is no instant cure. Healing takes time, effort, and patience.

If you believe in the process, "healing" can surely take place. Self-destructive behavior will usually change as the "healing" continues. Your "injured child" will "heal" and help the adult "go against the grain," so as to eventually feel more comfortable when involved in healthy behavior and nurturing relationships. During your "healing" journey, choices that were habitual or felt comfortable that proved to be unhealthy and self-destructive will slowly change to choices that are healthy and productive. As you "go against the grain" in making those self-caring choices, they too will start to become habitual and more comfortable. Although difficult at first, how refreshing it will be on your "healing" journey to experience choices that start to feel natural and nurturing and turn out to be constructive and functional, rather than demeaning and self-destructive. The picture I hope to leave you with is one that, for most of us, started in childhood and progressed through adulthood. At any juncture, a person can begin the "healing" process as I have outlined in chapter fourteen. The time spent with your witness can take as little as a month or as much as a year or two. The main thing is to believe in and start the process. Again, let me emphasize that a good witness should be a good empathic listener. The "telling of the story," which in most cases is the experience of the trauma or traumas, is the key. As you "tell the story," the "healing" will take place. Believe in the process and you too will come out the other side ready to "go against the grain." Once those repressed feelings are released, which should happen as you "tell the story," "healing" will surely occur. It may take telling the same story many times before the repressed feelings are felt and released. Remember, as I stated previously, success does not occur overnight. Hopefully, your witness will consider it a privilege that you chose him or her to hear "your story."

I have been fortunate not only to have been able to "tell my story" to an empathic witness, but to have had the opportunity in many years of practice to be the witness to hundreds of "healing patients" telling me "their stories." I have also had the wonderful opportunity to hear from those same patients how they had changed and reversed their self-destructive behaviors. I now invite you to travel that thrilling, rewarding, and "healing" road that leads you, too, to begin "going against the grain"!

About the Author

 Mark Adams attended the University of Stony Brook at Stony Brook, N.Y. where he received his Master's Degree in Social Work. He thereafter went on to obtain his Clinical License to practice Psychotherapy and spent ten years as a Psychiatric Social Worker at Brunswick Psychiatric Hospital in Amityville, N.Y. where he attended to the needs of the mental health population. For the twenty years from 1984 to 2004, Mark had his own clinical psychotherapy practice in Commack, N.Y. where he dealt extensively with all types of cases, but primarily with trauma and PTSD(Post Traumatic Stress Disorder)

www.ingramcontent.com/pod-product-compliance
Lightning Source LLC
Chambersburg PA
CBHW021251280526
45784CB00005B/2331